MANIFESTATION JOURNAL FOR BLACK WOMEN

Manifestation Journal for
BLACK WOMEN

A Guided Journal for
Attracting the Life You Want

Ashley R. Oliver, Esq.

ROCKRIDGE
PRESS

To my bestie,
TAWANDA ASAMAOWEI,
the OG manifestation Black girl.
I'll miss you forever.
I see you in the stars.

For general information on our other products and services, please contact our Customer Care Department within the United States at (866) 744-2665, or outside the United States at (510) 253-0500.

Paperback ISBN: 978-1-68539-905-4

Manufactured in the United States of America

Interior and Cover Designer: Tricia Jang
Art Producer: Melissa Malinowsky
Editor: Van Van Cleave
Production Editor: Emily Sheehan
Production Manager: David Zapanta

Cover and interior illustrations by Shutterstock: © Natasha_Mor (silhouettes), © Plasteed (background pattern); author photo courtesy of Amani Nichae of Honeysage Photo Co.

10 9 8 7 6 5 4 3 2 1 0

This Journal Belongs To

_____

CONTENTS

AN INTRODUCTION TO MANIFESTATION FOR BLACK WOMEN

Hey, sis! I don't know how you stumbled upon this journal, but it must mean that you're curious about elevating some aspect of your life—and I'm honored we get to do this together! Before we take this journey, let me introduce myself: I'm Ashley, a registered yoga teacher who specializes in restorative wellness, especially for people of color. I have dark skin, big hair, and a curvy body. I didn't see many yoga teachers like me, so I became one. Professionally, I am a civil rights lawyer who works as a diversity director in corporate America, a space where Black women haven't traditionally been accepted. I fused my love for wellness with my passion for inclusion and created Yoga and Mahogany, my social media platform where I talk about revolutionary wellness.

To know me is to know that I am very practical. When I first heard about manifestation, it seemed a little too "woo-woo" for me. You think something, so it just happens? Nah. But my best friend insisted that it was deeper than that. She told me that it was about moving my anxiety and limiting beliefs out of my way so that I could be the boss that I always dreamed of. I rolled my eyes, but as I began journaling—and I have journaled every day for over four years now—I saw my life change. I saw my dreams come true as I learned to affirm myself.

As Black women with roots in African spirituality, we are familiar with manifestation and affirmation on an ancestral level. Even the Zulu word *ubuntu*, which translates to "I am because we are," is an affirmation founded on the interconnectedness of African spirituality. It is rooted in the belief that each person is connected to the sky, the earth, and the underworld, that we all carry divinity within us as our birthright. And even though you don't need to practice that spirituality or hold the religious beliefs of our ancestors, there is a divinity that lives within you simply because you are a Black woman.

Although all that is beautiful, you may want me to get to the point. *Girl, what is manifestation?* Manifestation, simply, is changing how you use the power of your actions, emotions, beliefs, and habits to create the reality you want to experience. It means putting intentional energy behind your goals to make them a reality. Manifestation is sometimes misunderstood as being a passive approach to life—saying you want something but doing nothing about it. But that is *not* manifestation. Manifestation is less about waiting and more about creating; manifestation is knowing that you are the creator of your own life, that you are shaping it actively.

As a Black woman, you have been manifesting your whole life, sis! There are structural systems, like racism and sexism, that have been put into place to make our lives less full, less rich, and less meaningful. You looked those systems in the face and still manifested happiness, love, financial success, and accomplishments. All the goals and intentions that you made clear in hopes of creating a new reality for yourself— that's not just Black girl magic; that's manifestation!

So, because you're not entirely new to this, our time together is going to be spent harnessing that power—both ancestral and personal— to create a more intentional, confident mindset. It will remind you that despite the limitations the world may place on you, you are the creative director of your life, and you are creating a masterpiece!

HOW TO USE THIS JOURNAL

L ike your manifestation journey, how you use this journal is completely up to you. If you want to work through it page by page, that's fine. If you're more interested in prompts about money or want to try a specific practice in your real life, you can bounce around.

Part 1 will focus on discovering the life you want. At your own pace, you will go through the sections "Choosing the Life You Desire," "Overcoming Self-Doubt and Claiming Your Power," "Embracing Mindfulness and Gratitude," and "Setting Goals and Intentions." Part 2 will focus on manifesting the life you want, and you'll have space to track and reflect on the dreams and goals you are manifesting with care.

In this journal, there are four elements that will stretch you in different ways. First are affirmations. Affirmations are positive statements that combat negative thoughts and are easily repeatable. Second, there are prompts. Prompts are questions or statements to get your inner wheels turning and your soul stirring. Third, you'll have practices: actions you can take outside of journaling in this beautiful book. Last, there are interactive exercises to help you grow. I suggest trying all of them and taking note of any that particularly resonate with you.

PART 1

DISCOVERING THE LIFE YOU WANT

I owe it to my ancestors and myself to discover unyielding joy in this lifetime.

Choosing the Life You Desire

In this section, you will be exercising your mind, body, and soul to get to the truth about the life you truly desire. To me, one of the special things about being a Black woman is our resiliency. If something in our lives isn't working, we know how to pivot, honey! I want you to be honest with yourself about what you truly want next—not what your mama wants or what your homegirl wants, just you—and I want you to remind yourself that you, not other people, are the creator of your destiny. Many Black women are often so wildly busy that making time to dream and plan without someone or something needing their attention seems impossible. However, I believe that the more time you take to envision your new life, the more attainable that life will be. If you want to spin the block on an old goal, or go full speed ahead toward a new venture, now is the time to be explicit with your desires so that you can manifest them with intention. This is your journal, so don't hold back!

Living the same day over and over is boring, boo! Excitement is within reach. It's at the end of your comfort zone—but that doesn't mean it's not scary to venture that way. So, I have to ask: Have you ventured out of your comfort zone in the past month? If so, what did that experience teach you? What comfort zone do you plan to challenge next?

_____

_____

_____

_____

_____

_____

_____

_____

_____

_____

_____

_____

_____

_____

_____

_____

As a brilliant Black woman, I see the world is filled with endless opportunities for me.

BELLY BREATHING

The more stressful our day gets, especially when we are trying to plan our future, the shallower our breathing becomes. When we're stressed, we breathe from the throat and chest. But when we practice belly breathing, we engage our parasympathetic nervous system, and our chill mode is activated. The following technique stimulates those relaxation vibes, and if you're able to relax, then you can think more clearly and intentionally. Let's try it together:

1. Place your left hand over your heart and lovingly place your right hand over your belly.

2. Inhale through your nose slowly, filling your belly with air.

3. Purse your lips and exhale slowly, letting your belly deflate.

4. Repeat this cycle as needed.

Come back to this exercise when you're stressed. Take all the time you need, sis.

Say you are walking down the street after a great brunch, and you run into a homegirl you haven't seen in over a decade. After you exchange big hugs, she asks, "What have you been up to over the last ten years?" How would you answer her? What one tidbit would you be tempted to embellish?

_____

_____

_____

_____

_____

_____

_____

_____

_____

_____

_____

_____

_____

_____

_____

_____

_____

HAVE AND HAVE-NOTS

Sis, you know that if your mental health is lacking, it's so much harder to think affirmatively about the goals you want to achieve. We have to take care of ourselves! Although I recommend you speak to your physician or a mental health practitioner about your personal regimen, when I am feeling out of sorts, I pull out this checklist. I often find that missing just one item on this checklist can cause my vibe to be out of whack. When you're feeling out of sorts, answer the questions below:

1. Have I been getting six to eight hours of sleep lately?   Y   N

2. Have I eaten something substantive today?   Y   N

3. Have I recently talked to someone who loves me?   Y   N

4. Have I intentionally moved my body lately?   Y   N

5. Have I drunk water within the last two hours?   Y   N

6. Have I spent more than two hours a day on social media?   Y   N

7. Have I written down one thing I'm grateful for in the last day?   Y   N

Think of the most amazing Black woman you know—the type of Black woman who makes you sit up straight when she enters a room. What five qualities do you admire most about her? How could you implement those qualities in your life?

_____

_____

_____

_____

_____

_____

_____

_____

_____

_____

_____

_____

_____

_____

_____

_____

_____

I am the perfect age and the perfect size, and this is the perfect time to change my life.

HOT-GIRL MINDFULNESS WALK

It's no secret that walking helps your physical health, but let's talk about how walking with a purpose is dope for your mental health, too. Adding movement into your daily routine allows you to incorporate mindfulness as you focus on your body in the present moment. For your hot-girl walk, grab a water bottle, and head outside if you can. When you're outside, you can:

- enjoy a vibrant playlist (or listen to nature around you)
- feel the pavement below your feet
- pay attention to your body's pace and rhythm
- commit to a goal that you want to accomplish over the next day
- express gratitude to your body for carrying you through this exercise

There are no specific movements to remember, and you are not looking to achieve a certain physical expression. The only goal in walking is to be present, grateful, and goal-oriented!

You hit the jackpot! Your prize? A one-year, all-expenses-paid vacation to do whatever you want. If you didn't have to work for a year or worry about other people's opinions, what would you do?

_____

_____

_____

_____

_____

_____

_____

_____

_____

_____

_____

_____

_____

_____

_____

_____

_____

_____

_____

_____

_____

CREW LOVE

No sista is an island. To thrive as a Black woman, you need to have a well-balanced crew who sees the brilliance and beauty in you as you climb higher. It takes a village of all types of queens. Who is in yours? Being clear on the kinds of relationships you have with different women can help you manage your friendships. Let's consider those relationships:

1. When I need to vent about my day, I turn to

   _____ .

2. When I want to plan my next big career move, I reach out to

   _____ .

3. When I need to laugh until my sides hurt, I call

   _____ .

4. When I want to plan a fabulous trip, I travel with

   _____ .

5. When I need someone to tell me about myself, I listen to

   _____ .

Living through a pandemic has quite a way of making you reassess your priorities. What has become more important to you and your peace of mind since 2020? What has become less important or relevant to you since 2020?

_____

_____

_____

_____

_____

_____

_____

_____

_____

_____

_____

_____

_____

_____

_____

_____

_____

_____

_____

I enthusiastically
accept radical
responsibility for
creating the life
I desire.

RECLAIMING YOUR (SOCIAL MEDIA) TIME

There's nothing like minding your business on social media and then seeing a post that kills your vibe. Social media has been around for a long time so it's not unusual to have been following people for over a decade. Sometimes we keep connections with people out of habit or because we are curious, which is relatively harmless. But if you find yourself constantly comparing your life to the carefully curated digital lives of people online, and feeling envious or insignificant, it may be time to make a sweep of your digital space. The more positive your spaces are, the more positive your outlook will be in general. To do some social media cleansing today, go through your friends list and ask yourself the following questions.

- Is this a person from grade school or college whom I never really liked?

- Is this person an ex-partner or a close loved one of an ex?

- Does this person generally make me feel like I lack something or need to buy something?

- Is this person a former friend I'm keeping tabs on?

- Has it been a long time since this person brought any value or inspiration to my life?

If you answered yes to any of these questions, it's worth considering unfollowing that person—your peace of mind comes first!

Have you ever had one of those mornings when you wake up and do all the habits that get your self-care engine running, and you feel unstoppable? I love those mornings! What everyday habits make you feel like a force? List seven of them.

_____

_____

_____

_____

_____

_____

_____

_____

_____

_____

_____

_____

_____

_____

_____

_____

_____

_____

NOW AND WHEN

Being realistic and honest about who you are in this moment will bring you closer to the clarity you need to become the woman you want to be. Today, fill out the following chart to envision the steps you can take. In the first column, list ten words that describe your current self. In the middle column, list ten words that you'd like to use to describe yourself in the future. In the last column, list how you plan to turn those future descriptors into your reality.

CURRENT SELF	FUTURE SELF	HOW TO BECOME HER
1		
2		
3		
4		

5		
6		
7		
8		
9		
10		

Overcoming Self-Doubt and Claiming Your Power

Listen, you cannot keep doubting yourself! In a world where we are constantly fed a diet of fear, it's so easy to let self-doubt take over. But how can you manifest a different type of life if you don't trust your thoughts, your words, your actions, or your power? I'm not gonna lie to you—as someone who has dealt with anxiety most of her life, this is an everyday challenge for me, too. And, as Black women, we face structural hardship like racism and sexism that can make it even more challenging to tap into our power. But we aren't going to beat ourselves up for having doubt—it's natural to doubt. Instead, let's remember that doubt is just a little messenger reminding us that what we desire scares us a bit, and that's okay. In this section, we will feel the doubt, but we won't feed it, as we embrace the divinity that is our birthright as Black women. The following affirmations, prompts, practices, and exercises will encourage you to claim that power.

Trust is hard to build but easily lost, and we can even lose trust in ourselves. When do you feel that you trust yourself the most? On the flip side, when do you find it most difficult to trust yourself and your instincts?

_____

_____

_____

_____

_____

_____

_____

_____

_____

_____

_____

_____

_____

_____

_____

_____

_____

There are no limits
to my expanse. I'm a
Black queen; the world
is mine.

TWO-MINUTE PEP RALLY

Sometimes, you gotta break out your own pom-poms! Get out a pen and paper or your phone, put two minutes on the clock, and write a letter to yourself. Write like you are talking to a homegirl or a sister from the vantage point of a loved one who knows you and cares about you. I know you may not feel like the words you're writing are true, but practice makes perfect. After the two minutes are up, read the note aloud. Set a reminder for yourself to reread the note before bedtime as well.

Sometimes, we let the opinions of others (even our haters) impact the way we live our lives. Is there anything in your life that you would do differently if you didn't care about the opinions of others?

_____

_____

_____

_____

_____

_____

_____

_____

_____

_____

_____

_____

_____

_____

_____

_____

_____

_____

_____

_____

WILD, WILD THOUGHTS

Our negative thoughts, left unchecked, can feel like the Wild West—untamed and harmful. So, we're gonna lasso those thoughts and tell the truth to shame the devil! In the following table, write some of your negative thoughts. Be honest; this is your journal and no one else's. In the second column, make a rebuttal. Write down a specific incident that refutes that negative thought so you can see that your negative thoughts are lying to you. Here's an example from my life:

NEGATIVE THOUGHT	POSITIVE COUNTERSTATEMENT(S) OR EVENT
"I'm so annoying. No one wants to talk to me."	I just received a text from a friend from college this morning.

Our brains have a built-in negativity bias, which means they're built to register more negative stimuli. So it's even more important—and challenging—to intentionally think positive thoughts. What's one thought that has been getting the best of you lately? How has that thought shown up in your actions or inactions?

I am the master of
my own fate. I am
in total control of
my beautiful life.

When we're not acting with our own power, often we subconsciously wait for others to give us permission to do things. Is there something you want to do and are waiting to get the green light to accomplish? How can you give the power back to yourself to act?

_____

_____

_____

_____

_____

_____

_____

_____

_____

_____

_____

_____

_____

_____

_____

_____

_____

_____

WHAT'S YOUR FLAVOR?

What are the things that get you going? What excites you? What motivates you? What are you passionate about? For most of us, the things we are passionate about are our strengths, and when you tend to your strengths, your self-doubt doesn't have much to hold on to because you're too busy feeling yourself. Brainstorm your passions and your strengths. How can you intentionally incorporate your strengths this week? For each day on the following calendar, write an action item featuring a strength or passion of yours. For example, one of my strengths is mentorship. I plan to reach out on Monday to a local organization that mentors Black girls so I can be of service.

PASSIONS AND STRENGTHS

MON	
TUES	

WED	
THURS	
FRI	
SAT	
SUN	

SURF THE URGE

The idea of urge surfing originated with clinical psychologist Dr. G. Alan Marlatt. It's helpful in overcoming addictive behaviors that are limiting your power, such as checking your social media too much or eating mindlessly. Whenever you're feeling an urge to do something you know isn't beneficial to you, do this:

1. Focus on the area where you are having the craving.

2. Acknowledge how you are experiencing the craving.

3. Take deep breaths to release tension.

4. Repeat, focusing on the area where you are experiencing the craving.

How we perceive our bodies can dramatically affect our confidence. Without looking in the mirror, name five of your favorite physical traits. List why they are your favorites.

_____

_____

_____

_____

_____

_____

_____

_____

_____

_____

_____

_____

_____

_____

_____

_____

_____

_____

_____

Every experience,
good and bad,
shapes me into an
unstoppable force.

CHART TOPPER

In this practice, you're gonna write down your own personal top twenty hits. On a piece of paper, create two columns. In the first column, in chronological order, write down twenty of your accomplishments. In the second column, write down some affirmations that are based on what you accomplished. Here's an example:

Accomplishment: *I wrote for the state newspaper at the age of ten.*

Affirmation: *I have had ambition and excellence instilled in me since I was a young girl.*

Don't forget—your accomplishments can also be things that you didn't let defeat you. Here's another personal example:

Accomplishment: *My anxiety was crippling my first year in college, but I stayed in school.*

Affirmation: *I meet unknown challenges head-on, and I still succeed.*

SING IT, SIS!

So many amazing Black women artists have shared their journeys of overcoming self-doubt and claiming their power through their gift of song. Today, let their words encourage you and remind you that you aren't alone. Find a playlist of Black women singers or rappers that you admire, then write down the powerful or inspirational lyrics you relate to.

NAME OF ARTIST	NAME OF SONG	LYRICS

NAME OF ARTIST	NAME OF SONG	LYRICS

What are three feel-good activities that make you forget any insecurities you may have about your body and that make you feel less self-conscious? How can you incorporate them into your schedule?

_____

_____

_____

_____

_____

_____

_____

_____

_____

_____

_____

_____

_____

_____

_____

_____

_____

Embracing Mindfulness and Gratitude

I t may seem a little counterintuitive in a manifestation journal where we are striving for the future to have a whole chapter focused on the present, but I can assure you that it's not. Being grateful for what you have right now and cultivating that attitude of gratitude is essential to manifesting your ideal future. Gratitude is all about being aware of what you have, instead of focusing on what you lack, and appreciating what is going well, instead of dwelling on what is going wrong. When you're mindful of your present circumstances and the bounties and blessings you have now, you are more hopeful, positive, and intentional about attracting even more amazing experiences in the future. I have written in my personal gratitude journal every day for the past four years, and the abundant harvest I've received just by being grateful for seedlings of joy has shocked me! In this section, we're gonna bloom where we are planted and embrace what we have with some affirmations, prompts, practices, and exercises, all geared toward gratitude.

As a modern Black woman, you probably don't have much time for mindfulness. Take a deep breath (seriously, right now!). Ask yourself: "What do I need in this moment?" The answer may surprise you. Then ask yourself: "What can I do to honor that request?"

_____

_____

_____

_____

_____

_____

_____

_____

_____

_____

_____

_____

_____

_____

_____

_____

_____

_____

_____

I grant myself
permission to be
still and present
and to rest.

TOO LEGIT

Write down two people or things you love, such as a close friend or your cozy bedroom. Next, write down two positive emotions you want to experience today. Then, plug your words into this affirmational statement:

Even though the day is just starting, I'm already feeling

_____ *(positive emotion 1).*

And when I think about how lucky I am to have

_____ *(person/thing 1)*

and _____ *(person/thing 2)*

in my life, I am filled with so much gratitude! No matter what

happens today, I'm feeling _____ *(positive emotion 2)*

because I am fortunate in so many ways.

Every morning, play around with your word combinations until you have an affirmational statement that helps you feel grateful. The combinations are endless!

So many of us have horror stories about work (e.g., miscommunication between coworkers, missed deadlines, microaggressions). But sometimes a terrible situation at work can become an amazing opportunity for growth down the road. Write about a career setback that actually turned out to be a setup for success.

_____

_____

_____

_____

_____

_____

_____

_____

_____

_____

_____

_____

_____

_____

_____

_____

_____

_____

I COULD GO ON AND ON

Gratitude is an attitude, but it's also a practice. The more you practice, the more natural it will become. Each day for the next twenty-one days, write three things you are grateful for—one in the morning, one in the afternoon, and one at night. Why twenty-one days? Research shows it takes about that amount of time for the brain to form a new habit, which it can do because of its neuroplasticity.

Over the twenty-one days, try not to repeat an entry. Also, I want to remind you that the thing you're grateful for doesn't have to be big. If you're grateful for a fresh cup of coffee, that's fine! I recommend setting an alarm or an alert on your calendar to remind you to write each entry. It's okay if it feels hard at first. Over time, you'll find that your brain will naturally start to look for things to be grateful for each day.

1	2	3

4	5	6
7	8	9

CONTINUED →

10	11	12

13	14	15

16	17	18
19	20	21

Think about the ways you care for a loved one. Do you give them gifts or maybe perform errands for them? Do you surprise them with thoughtful texts? Now, flip it and think of yourself as your own loved one. How do you care for yourself? What are some other ways you can do so?

_____

_____

_____

_____

_____

_____

_____

_____

_____

_____

_____

_____

_____

_____

_____

_____

I am present in
this moment. I am
safe in my beautiful
Black body.

FOUR-PAGE LETTER

Expressing gratitude for others is dope because it helps you feel more positively about yourself, increases social bonds, and makes you happier. Think about someone you are deeply grateful for but to whom you've never expressed how you feel. It can be anyone but preferably someone that you can reach quickly, either in person or online. Then, write them a letter using the following guidelines:

- Address the person directly in your salutation. Be as formal or informal as you'd like.

- Tell them specific things about their personality, your relationship, and/or your experience with them that have influenced your life.

- Let them know why, out of everyone in the world, you decided to write a letter to them.

When you're done, send the letter in the mail, through email, or on social media. Don't worry about whether it's perfect; it's the thought that counts. Bonus points for bravery if you deliver the letter in person, particularly if it's someone you've lost touch with.

As the years pass, we get more than gray hair; we also get some wisdom. What is something that you are more grateful for as time passes? (For me, it's the peace and quiet of Christmas evening.)

_____

_____

_____

_____

_____

_____

_____

_____

_____

_____

_____

_____

_____

_____

_____

_____

_____

_____

FLIP IT AND REVERSE IT

Have you ever had something that you wanted go so completely wrong that it actually turned into what you needed? Sometimes a no right now sets the stage for a YASSSSSS later. One sign of emotional maturity is being able to discern when our plans may not have been the best in the long run. List ten experiences with outcomes that you did not want but that turned out to be exactly what you needed, either in that moment or later. Here's my example: I'm grateful that I didn't get that job in Tennessee because I never would have met my husband in Kentucky.

1. I'm grateful _____

   because _____.

2. I'm grateful _____

   because _____.

3. I'm grateful _____

   because _____.

4. I'm grateful _____

   because _____.

5. I'm grateful _____

   because _____.

6. I'm grateful _____

    because _____.

7. I'm grateful _____

    because _____.

8. I'm grateful _____

    because _____.

9. I'm grateful _____

    because _____.

10. I'm grateful _____

    because _____.

Sometimes, when we think of gratitude, we feel like we have to focus on the big things. But the small everyday joys are just as important! Write down seven little joys that make your day. (One of mine? A cherry Tootsie Pop.)

_____

_____

_____

_____

_____

_____

_____

_____

_____

_____

_____

_____

_____

_____

_____

_____

_____

_____

I am grateful for
opposition because it
makes me stronger.

BALANCING ACT

What I love about yoga is that it requires mindfulness to do the poses correctly. There's no pose more foundational than the tree pose, so today, give it a try using the following steps.

1. Stand and inhale deeply. Lift your chest.

2. Find a small dot on the floor about six feet in front of you and stare at it to help you balance.

3. Settle your weight onto your left leg, and slowly guide your right foot to the inside of your ankle, leg, or knee. If it is uncomfortable to stand on one leg, feel free to sit with your left leg extended and your right knee bent so that the bottom of your foot is against the inside of your left leg in a pike formation.

4. Turn your right knee out to open up your hips, and bring your palms together.

5. Continue to stare at the small dot on the floor. Try to maintain your balance for five full breaths (inhales and exhales).

6. When finished, slowly lower your arms and legs, then shake them out.

7. Repeat steps 3 through 6 with your weight on your right leg.

Not everyone has the pleasure and honor of being a Black woman. Today, reflect on our culture and lineage, then write down five things that make you grateful to be a Black woman.

_____

_____

_____

_____

_____

_____

_____

_____

_____

_____

_____

_____

_____

_____

_____

_____

_____

_____

IT'S ALL IN YOUR HEAD

Mindfulness can seem really intimidating, but there are a host of games and activities that require concentration and staying in the present moment—that's mindfulness! Here's a checklist of activities that help improve your focus and strengthen your mindfulness muscle. Check off the ones that are your favorites and the ones that you're interested in trying out.

☐ Coloring in adult coloring books

☐ Playing Jenga

☐ Lying in the grass

☐ Listening to wind chimes

☐ Practicing belly breathing

☐ Playing catch

☐ Playing Simon Says

☐ Doing yoga poses

☐ Walking mindfully

☐ Blowing bubbles

☐ Writing with your nondominant hand

☐ Looking through a new window

☐ Learning a new dance

☐ Practicing guided meditations

☐ Creating with Play-Doh

☐ Singing (loudly) the lyrics to your favorite song

Setting Goals and Intentions

All right, sis! We're feeling more confident, and we've honed in on our desires, so now it's time to take all that information and put it in motion by setting goals and intentions. First of all, I want to remind you that you are a queen, and, therefore, the "rules" of goal setting don't apply to you— you're not limited to creating goals only on New Year's Eve or at the beginning of each quarter. Any day—every day—is a great time to map out your goals! And if the goals you set last year or last week don't work, you are free to change your mind without shame or judgment. When it comes to manifesting the life you want, it's imperative that you have a great intention-setting practice. Goals are more external and focused on the future, but intentions are set in the present, focused on an internal state of being, and can be affirmed (and practiced) daily. In this section, we'll work through affirmations, prompts, practices, and exercises designed to pique your curiosity about your future and help you set goals and intentions for what you hope to manifest.

The library is open! Reading challenges us and nurtures our curiosity. What's the last book you read that was related to your career progression? What three things did you learn from it? How can you apply those lessons to your career goals?

_____

_____

_____

_____

_____

_____

_____

_____

_____

_____

_____

_____

_____

_____

_____

_____

_____

I can withstand discomfort. All my goals exist outside my comfort zone.

SAFE SPACE

Creating a safe and/or sacred space in your home makes it easier to take off the day's armor and set intentions. Today, choose a location in your house you'd like to upgrade. Pick a space that is tucked away, like a nook or an empty closet. Then, use your five senses to decorate it using stuff from around your crib:

Touch: Grab a comfy pillow or two. Include textures that ground you, such as a silk sheet. Then, add adornments that are meaningful to you, whether they are spiritual or aesthetic, such as crystals or prayer beads.

Hear: Set up a small speaker, if possible, to play white or brown noise or peaceful music.

Smell: Try candles or incense in scents you find grounding.

Taste: Grab a cup of water, a cup of hot tea, or a yummy snack with a pleasant texture to bring into your space.

See: Last, add plants or flowers, a serene backdrop, or photos that make you smile.

Over the next few days, enjoy your safe space whenever you need a break.

So you wake up after eight hours of incredible dream-inducing sleep—now what? A morning routine catered to your personal rhythm and needs is an important way to start a successful day. What is your current morning routine? Does it set you up for success? What other habits can you incorporate?

_____

_____

_____

_____

_____

_____

_____

_____

_____

_____

_____

_____

_____

_____

_____

_____

YOUR MASTER-CLASS MOMENT

You've seen those interviews before: A brilliant, accomplished, successful person sits down on a swanky set with an award-winning journalist to tell the world exactly how they became so brilliant, so accomplished, and so successful.

Now it's your time to shine. Imagine that your glam team just left the stage after finishing the final touches and the journalist, beaming with anticipation, asks you, "So, everyone knows about the goal you set five years ago, and now, here you are! How did you do it?"

On the following lines, write out how you would answer this question. What was the goal? How did you change your life in five years? Reverse engineering your goals in this way can be an illuminating (and fun!) way to gain insight into how your mind breaks down complex tasks.

_____

_____

_____

_____

_____

_____

_____

_____

_____

_____

"Service is the rent we pay for being," the brilliant Black woman activist Marian Wright Edelman once penned. When our goals are tied to societal aims, we often feel a deeper sense of connectedness. What community-wide or worldwide goals do you want your work to be in service of?

_____

_____

_____

_____

_____

_____

_____

_____

_____

_____

_____

_____

_____

_____

_____

_____

My progress
won't be linear, but
each step I take
toward growth is
still progress.

THESE ARE MY INTENTIONS

Many people set goals, but setting intentions is different. A goal focuses on the future; an intention focuses on this present moment. Goals are destinations or specific achievements. Intentions exist daily, no matter whether you achieve the goal or reach the destination. To live a more intention-filled life, we can reverse engineer our goals to create our intentions.

In your safe space, write down a goal, then take a moment to reflect on what this goal says about your current desires (intentions). Here's an example:

Goal: I want to walk for thirty minutes a day, every day.

Intention: I am in tune with my body, and I take care of it.

_____

_____

Continue writing down as many goals and intentions as you want. When you have a list you're satisfied with, set a timeline for starting and completing your goals.

_____

_____

_____

_____

_____

Sometimes we sabotage our own goals because we know they will require leaving some version of ourselves behind. And that feels hella vulnerable because we don't know what's on the other side. What habits, relationships, or excuses are you holding on to that are keeping you from accomplishing your goals?

_____

_____

_____

_____

_____

_____

_____

_____

_____

_____

_____

_____

_____

_____

_____

_____

_____

_____

THIS PERFECTLY ORDINARY DAY

Life has its ups and downs, but most of us aspire for ordinary days with a little razzle-dazzle. Today, write down what your perfect—but ordinary—day would look and feel like. Some rules: On your perfectly ordinary day, you're not on vacation, there's no unusual decadence, and there's no sudden windfall of money. Answer the following questions to outline the type of day you wouldn't mind repeating over and over.

What is your perfect but ordinary morning routine after waking up?

_____

_____

What is your perfect but ordinary breakfast?

_____

_____

What is your perfect but ordinary workday?

_____

_____

What is your perfect but ordinary communication with your loved ones?

_____

_____

What is your perfect but ordinary lunch schedule?

_____

_____

What is your perfect but ordinary self-care routine?

_____

_____

What are your perfect but ordinary dinner and evening plans?

_____

_____

What is your perfect but ordinary bedtime routine?

_____

_____

Let's keep it real, sis: You're not going to accomplish every goal. So, let's prepare for that. How can you best accept not meeting a particular goal? If you did not meet a goal, how can you use that as positive fuel for future aspirations?

_____

_____

_____

_____

_____

_____

_____

_____

_____

_____

_____

_____

_____

_____

_____

_____

_____

_____

I am a soul with
good intentions.
My intentions
are the soil for
fertile dreams.

TAKE BACK THE NIGHT

Anytime is a great time to set intentions, but setting intentions at night, right before you drift off to sleep, allows you to influence your subconscious mind more directly, according to an article in the journal *Sleep*. Here is a quick exercise to do right before you go to sleep:

Think of one person in your world who needs more love. Picture them in your mind. Breathe deeply. Send them love.

Think of a part of your body that needs extra kindness. Breathe deeply. Touch that part. Send it kindness.

Think of a past version of yourself who needed more grace. Breathe deeply. Place your hand on your heart. Send that past version of yourself grace.

Think of one short intention to lead you into the next day, such as "I am attracting kindness." Say it aloud, and drift off to sleep.

Home is where the heart is. It's also where your peace is and where you can optimally recharge away from the world. What does your dream home look like? Who lives in it, and where is it located? If it's your current home (how lucky!), how would you like to improve it?

_____

_____

_____

_____

_____

_____

_____

_____

_____

_____

_____

_____

_____

_____

_____

_____

_____

_____

FORGET-ME-NOT

We've heard that our phones are super distracting and lead to deep bouts of unproductivity. That's definitely fair, but you can also use your phone's powers for good!

In the following chart, write out up to ten behavior reminders tied to goals you want to accomplish. Then write out the frequency you'll need those reminders.

Once you're finished, add the reminders to your phone through a calendar or notes app to give you a boost of encouragement throughout the day. This is one of my favorite tricks to stay on top of my goals and get the extra push I need to accomplish them.

Here's one of my reminders: "I love that you're drinking your water and stretching your body, sis!" I set that reminder to occur twice daily: at 10 a.m., after my morning meeting, and at 3 p.m., when I'm feeling a little sluggish at work.

BEHAVIOR REMINDERS	FREQUENCY OF REMINDERS
1.	

CONTINUED →

BEHAVIOR REMINDERS	FREQUENCY OF REMINDERS
2.	
3.	
4.	
5.	

BEHAVIOR REMINDERS	FREQUENCY OF REMINDERS
6.	
7.	
8.	
9.	

PART 2

MANIFESTING THE LIFE YOU WANT

I generously give myself
the grace to grow and manifest
the life I desire.

DATE: _____

I'M GRATEFUL FOR: _____

I'M MANIFESTING: _____

_____

_____

When was the last time someone told you (or you told yourself) to be strong? What emotions were you not allowed to express? How do you plan to respond next time?

_____

_____

_____

_____

_____

As a Black woman, I am entitled to all my emotions.

DATE: _____

I'M GRATEFUL FOR: _____

I'M MANIFESTING: _____

_____

_____

Who your homies are matters! What relationships in your life fill you up and why? What relationships drain your energy? Write down why you're not feeling it.

_____

_____

_____

_____

_____

My loved ones will lift me up when life is heavy. I am my community.

DATE: _____

I'M GRATEFUL FOR: _____

I'M MANIFESTING: _____

_____

_____

Have you ever met someone who doesn't take any mess from anyone? That self-assurance is goals! Whom do you know who is like that? What habits of theirs would you like to emulate?

_____

_____

_____

_____

_____

I see inspirational people all around me. I am enriched by my circle.

DATE: _____

I'M GRATEFUL FOR: _____

I'M MANIFESTING: _____

_____

_____

Is there any part of you that needs more compassion and kindness?
Write a note to yourself to read when you need to re-up that self-love.

_____

_____

_____

_____

_____

I permit myself to put myself first. Self-compassion is my birthright.

DATE: _____

I'M GRATEFUL FOR: _____

I'M MANIFESTING: _____

_____

_____

Have you ever fallen short when a homegirl needed you? It happens, sis! What happened? How would you have responded if you were in her place? How do you plan to show up differently next time?

_____

_____

_____

_____

_____

> ## I am surrounded by beautiful Black queens who can rely on my sisterhood.

DATE: _____

I'M GRATEFUL FOR: _____

I'M MANIFESTING: _____

_____

_____

If you had a million dollars in your account to back a brilliant idea, what business related to your passion or expertise would you create?

_____

_____

_____

_____

_____

I can turn my innate and learned expertise into increased and sustainable income.

DATE: _____

I'M GRATEFUL FOR: _____

I'M MANIFESTING: _____

_____

_____

Relax, relate, release! Is there a decision you've made in the past that you're ashamed of? How would it feel to let go of that shame?

_____

_____

_____

_____

_____

I am bigger than shame.
I extend to myself the same grace
I would offer a friend.

I'M GRATEFUL FOR: _____

I'M MANIFESTING: _____

_____

_____

Girl, people continue trying you! What are five surefire ways that you can calm yourself down in a frustrating situation instead of turning it up?

_____

_____

_____

_____

_____

I can always choose
the peace within me and ignore
the chaos around me.

I'M GRATEFUL FOR: _____

I'M MANIFESTING: _____

_____

_____

What was a situation where someone took advantage of your kindness—mentally, emotionally, physically, or financially? How would you hold them accountable now?

_____

_____

_____

_____

_____

I forgive myself for accepting less. I now know my worth, and I add tax.

DATE: _____

I'M GRATEFUL FOR: _____

I'M MANIFESTING: _____

_____

_____

Many Black women have a "hair story." Where are you on your journey with your hair? Are you in a different place than you were as a young child?

_____

_____

_____

_____

_____

My hair is gravity defying and gorgeous. My kinks and curls are incredible.

DATE: _____

I'M GRATEFUL FOR: _____

I'M MANIFESTING: _____
_____
_____

No is a full sentence, but it can be hard to hold that line. Write down some responses to use when someone keeps pressing you after you establish a boundary.

_____
_____
_____
_____
_____

I allow myself to say no.
My time and my energy
belong only to me.

DATE: _____

I'M GRATEFUL FOR: _____

I'M MANIFESTING: _____

_____

_____

Push it! What new goals or new experiences are you excited to embark on? What steps do you need to take to get there? Which sis can you rely on to hold you accountable to your goal?

_____

_____

_____

_____

_____

I can accomplish anything. Nothing is impossible for a woman like me.

DATE: _____

I'M GRATEFUL FOR: _____

I'M MANIFESTING: _____

_____

_____

Turn up! It's your one hundredth birthday. Everyone is there, and the speeches are flowing. What events or experiences would you want people to share about the life you've lived?

_____

_____

_____

_____

_____

I have ancestors who are rooting
for me and conspiring in my favor.

DATE: _____

I'M GRATEFUL FOR: _____

I'M MANIFESTING: _____

_____

_____

What gets your creative juices flowing? Write down a list of things that make you feel both competent and creative. Can you incorporate one of these practices into your week?

_____

_____

_____

_____

_____

I am a creative dynamo, overflowing with an abundance of ideas.

DATE: _____

I'M GRATEFUL FOR: _____

I'M MANIFESTING: _____

_____

_____

Cover girl! Your absolute favorite magazine is writing a story about you. If they wrote it today, what would the story be? What would change if they wrote a follow-up next year?

_____

_____

_____

_____

_____

> ## I am a Black woman, so I am naturally influential. I am always the trend.

DATE: _____

I'M GRATEFUL FOR: _____

I'M MANIFESTING: _____

_____

_____

When was the last time you allowed someone to support you emotionally? What was the situation? If it's been a long time, how can you practice being more vulnerable?

_____

_____

_____

_____

_____

My community will show up for me when I need them because I matter.

DATE: _____

I'M GRATEFUL FOR: _____

I'M MANIFESTING: _____

_____

_____

As a child, what were you taught a successful life looked like?
Do you still hold some of those thoughts? If not, how do you define a
successful life now?

_____

_____

_____

_____

_____

I will be my own version of successful, peaceful, and happy— not anyone else's.

DATE: _____

I'M GRATEFUL FOR: _____

I'M MANIFESTING: _____

_____

_____

Sis, are you getting paid what you're worth? Are there areas where you aren't being compensated fairly for your experience or expertise? How can you advocate for an increase?

_____

_____

_____

_____

_____

My inherent expertise and experience will always lead to abundance.

DATE: _____

I'M GRATEFUL FOR: _____

I'M MANIFESTING: _____

_____

_____

Being able to self-soothe—to calm yourself in times of stress—is an incredible superpower. What are your three favorite ways to self-soothe? What do you tell yourself when you need to heal?

_____

_____

_____

_____

_____

I allow myself to feel deep emotions because I trust myself to heal.

DATE: _____

I'M GRATEFUL FOR: _____

I'M MANIFESTING: _____

_____

_____

Perfection is the enemy of progress. If you tussle with perfectionism, what do you think is driving it? If negative thoughts stemming from perfectionism start to creep in, how can you respond?

_____

_____

_____

_____

_____

I can withstand uncertainty
because I know I can meet
any challenge.

DATE: _____

I'M GRATEFUL FOR: _____

I'M MANIFESTING: _____

_____

_____

What was the toughest time in your life—a time that you thought you weren't gonna make it through? What did you learn about yourself during that experience?

_____

_____

_____

_____

_____

I have survived every
tough moment in my life.
I can withstand anything.

DATE: _____

I'M GRATEFUL FOR: _____

I'M MANIFESTING: _____

_____

_____

What's a topic that you are really tough on yourself about? Write yourself a personal permission slip that gives you grace to not be so tough on yourself.

_____

_____

_____

_____

_____

I can release myself from shame. On the other side of shame is divine healing.

DATE: _____

I'M GRATEFUL FOR: _____

I'M MANIFESTING: _____

_____

_____

Feeling emotion is healthy . . . and exhausting. Which emotion are you most uncomfortable sitting with? Which emotions do you actively try to avoid?

_____

_____

_____

_____

_____

I am in control of my emotions. I permit myself to feel them and move through them.

DATE: _____

I'M GRATEFUL FOR: _____

I'M MANIFESTING: _____

_____

_____

Ever wish you had a time machine? If you had an extra hour added to each day, what would you do with it (excluding sleeping and eating)?

_____

_____

_____

_____

_____

I am walking into a transformational season of my life. I am that girl.

DATE: _____

I'M GRATEFUL FOR: _____

I'M MANIFESTING: _____

_____

_____

Are you a master procrastinator? What are you putting off right now? Why do you think you're doing so? How would you encourage a home-girl going through the same situation?

_____

_____

_____

_____

_____

I can start now.
I can start over.
I can start when I'm ready.

DATE: _____

I'M GRATEFUL FOR: _____

I'M MANIFESTING: _____

_____

_____

It's giving, boss chick! When have you felt most successful? What situation—like saving for a down payment, establishing a wellness routine, working with a career coach, or climbing the ladder in your industry, for example—makes you feel most accomplished?

_____

_____

_____

_____

_____

I am that girl. My accomplishments inspire others. I am a role model.

DATE: _____

I'M GRATEFUL FOR: _____

I'M MANIFESTING: _____

_____

_____

Your inner child is asking you to come outside and play! What's one activity that you loved doing in your childhood? How can you incorporate it into your self-care routine?

_____

_____

_____

_____

_____

I am honored I get to be a
Black woman in this lifetime.
How divine!

I'M GRATEFUL FOR: _____

I'M MANIFESTING: _____

_____

_____

What are some songs that automatically put you in a good mood?
Write them down to make your personal happiness playlist. Which
lyrics could you repeat as affirmations?

_____

_____

_____

_____

_____

I will allow myself to experience
unrelenting joy! I deserve to play
and laugh.

DATE: _____

I'M GRATEFUL FOR: _____

I'M MANIFESTING: _____

_____

_____

Even queens have traits we're not too proud of. What are three of yours? Why and when did they develop?

_____

_____

_____

_____

_____

_____

I am patient with my journey. I
know that becoming my best self
takes time.

DATE: _____

I'M GRATEFUL FOR: _____

I'M MANIFESTING: _____

_____

_____

You wear it well! What is your favorite outfit—the one that makes you feel irresistible, powerful, or nostalgic? Why does that outfit make you feel this way?

_____

_____

_____

_____

_____

I look in the mirror, and I see
a powerful woman. I can wear
anything well.

DATE: _____

I'M GRATEFUL FOR: _____

I'M MANIFESTING: _____

_____

_____

Do you trust yourself to make decisions, or do you trust others' opinions more than your own? How would it feel to trust yourself first and foremost?

_____

_____

_____

_____

_____

I will stand by my decisions and trust my voice. They are safe and sound.

DATE: _____

I'M GRATEFUL FOR: _____

I'M MANIFESTING: _____

_____

_____

When you were a little girl, what did you want to be when you grew up? Does any part of you still carry that aspiration? How has it changed?

_____

_____

_____

_____

_____

I love the little girl in me.
She deserves to be seen
and heard.

DATE: _____

I'M GRATEFUL FOR: _____

I'M MANIFESTING: _____

_____

_____

There's nothing worse than losing money. Have you made money mistakes in the past? If so, what did you learn from them?

_____

_____

_____

_____

_____

My past does not dictate my
present abundance. I am attracting
riches and success.

DATE: _____

I'M GRATEFUL FOR: _____

I'M MANIFESTING: _____

_____

_____

Do you have any unfinished projects? List out a few of them, and then write out why they are unfinished. What can you do to breathe new life into them?

_____

_____

_____

_____

_____

I can take mere ideas and turn them into projects, businesses, and empires.

DATE: _____

I'M GRATEFUL FOR: _____

I'M MANIFESTING: _____

_____

_____

Our ancestors are always closer than we think. If you could talk to your ancestors and ask for guidance, what particular concerns or troubles would you need advice on?

_____

_____

_____

_____

_____

My ancestors are protecting me. I am never alone in the universe.

DATE: _____

I'M GRATEFUL FOR: _____

I'M MANIFESTING: _____

_____

_____

Do you allow yourself time to play, or are you more focused on being productive? What's one small playful act that you can implement in your schedule today?

_____

_____

_____

_____

_____

My laughter and my joy are my resistance to a system that wants me exhausted.

I'M GRATEFUL FOR: _____

I'M MANIFESTING: _____

_____

_____

How are you suppressing your emotions? Do you use social media, food, TV shows, or busyness to avoid them? How would it feel to experience those emotions for five minutes?

_____

_____

_____

_____

_____

I am bigger than my emotions. My emotions come and go; I outlast them all.

DATE: _____

I'M GRATEFUL FOR: _____

I'M MANIFESTING: _____

_____

_____

Is it hard or easy to express your boundaries to others? If it is hard, what's one small way you can practice expressing a boundary to others this week?

_____

_____

_____

_____

_____

My boundaries protect me
from chaos. My boundaries
keep peace close.

DATE: _____

I'M GRATEFUL FOR: _____

I'M MANIFESTING: _____

_____

_____

What was your favorite thing about your body when you were a Black child? How do you feel about that part of your body now? Has your perception changed?

_____

_____

_____

_____

_____

My body is constantly ebbing
and flowing. I will love it
through the changes.

DATE: _____

I'M GRATEFUL FOR: _____

I'M MANIFESTING: _____

_____

_____

Our attention spans are shorter than ever these days. What distractions are you allowing into your day? Are there ways you can reduce them?

_____

_____

_____

_____

_____

All the experiences I face
mold me into the best
version of myself.

I'M GRATEFUL FOR: _____

I'M MANIFESTING: _____

_____

_____

Sis, are you getting in your own way? If you knew you couldn't fail, what new skills and hobbies would you love to try? Why haven't you tried them yet?

_____

_____

_____

_____

_____

I have untapped creativity and genius. My well is endless, never dry.

DATE: _____

I'M GRATEFUL FOR: _____

I'M MANIFESTING: _____

_____

_____

Can a girl find some peace of mind? Peace can sometimes feel elusive, so let's define it. What thoughts, people, words, memories, music, places, or sounds convey the feeling of peace for you?

_____

_____

_____

_____

My peace of mind is a valuable gift. I deserve peace in a chaotic world.

DATE: _____

I'M GRATEFUL FOR: _____

I'M MANIFESTING: _____
_____
_____

We know that Black women are resilient, but do you actually believe you can do hard things? If not, what's something you can do to practice trusting your own power?

_____
_____
_____
_____
_____

Being a Black woman
is revolutionary. I was born
to overcome.

I'M GRATEFUL FOR: _____

I'M MANIFESTING: _____

_____

_____

Leisure is life's greatest luxury. Currently, how do you enjoy spending your free time? How would this change if all your financial needs were taken care of?

_____

_____

_____

_____

_____

I am permitted to be still. Resting is my birthright as a Black woman.

DATE: _____

I'M GRATEFUL FOR: _____

I'M MANIFESTING: _____

_____

_____

Who provides you with emotional safety—the ability to be open and vulnerable? What makes you trust this person? How do they impact your future growth and future goals?

_____

_____

_____

_____

_____

I attract people who love me,
see me, and fight for me.

DATE: _____

I'M GRATEFUL FOR: _____

I'M MANIFESTING: _____

_____

_____

Sometimes things don't work out. Do you feel disappointed by any outcomes right now? Instead of pushing the disappointment away, how does it feel to allow yourself space to experience it?

_____

_____

_____

_____

_____

I know that when things don't
work out in my favor, something
better is coming soon.

DATE: _____

I'M GRATEFUL FOR: _____

I'M MANIFESTING: _____

_____

_____

Being out in nature can help us practice mindfulness and stay in the present. What is your favorite place to be in nature? What do you appreciate most about it?

_____

_____

_____

_____

_____

My soul feels at peace when I'm in tune with nature. The earth is healing me.

DATE: _____

I'M GRATEFUL FOR: _____

I'M MANIFESTING: _____

_____

_____

Do you try to overly control the behaviors of yourself or others? No judgment. It happens! When you engage in controlling tendencies, what are you trying to hold on to?

_____

_____

_____

_____

_____

> I don't need to control the
> uncontrollable. I can withstand
> the uncertainty of life.

I'M GRATEFUL FOR: _____

I'M MANIFESTING: _____

_____

_____

Are you part of a relationship (romantic, friendship, work, etc.) that no longer serves you? What are your reasons for continuing the relationship? What would it take for you to leave?

_____

_____

_____

_____

_____

I am allowed to leave people and places that hurt me instead of heal me.

DATE: _____

I'M GRATEFUL FOR: _____

I'M MANIFESTING: _____

_____

_____

Believe the hype! What compliments do you receive over and over? Do you believe these compliments? If not, why not? What would it take to believe them?

_____

_____

_____

_____

_____

My inner glow is apparent to
those around me. I am worthy
of the praise.

DATE: _____

I'M GRATEFUL FOR: _____

I'M MANIFESTING: _____

_____

_____

What is the biggest promise you've made to yourself? Have you kept it? If not, what can you do now to keep that commitment to your future self?

_____

_____

_____

_____

_____

I deserve to put myself in a position to experience greatness.

DATE: _____

I'M GRATEFUL FOR: _____

I'M MANIFESTING: _____

_____

_____

Do you allow yourself to feel angry, or do you stifle the flames?
When was the last time you talked yourself down from expressing
your anger?

_____

_____

_____

_____

_____

My anger is righteous.
My anger protects me.
My anger has meaning.

DATE: _____

I'M GRATEFUL FOR: _____

I'M MANIFESTING: _____

_____

_____

When you think about your finances, how do you feel? Do you experience overwhelm, disappointment, contentment, or something else? Can you shift toward an abundance mindset, believing that money comes to you easily?

_____

_____

_____

_____

_____

I allow money to flow into my life with ease. I will always have enough.

DATE: _____

I'M GRATEFUL FOR: _____

I'M MANIFESTING: _____

_____

_____

There are a lot of fictional baddies we can learn from. If you were a fictional character from a book, TV show, or movie, who would you be and why?

_____

_____

_____

_____

_____

I seek inspiration to change my life from a plethora of sources.

DATE: _____

I'M GRATEFUL FOR: _____

I'M MANIFESTING: _____

_____

_____

Hey, girl! On the following lines, introduce yourself to your younger self. Which attributes about your current self would you emphasize? Which present traits would you be tempted to leave out?

_____

_____

_____

_____

_____

_____

I am constantly evolving, constantly changing, and constantly healing.

DATE: _____

I'M GRATEFUL FOR: _____

I'M MANIFESTING: _____

_____

_____

Do you define yourself by any of the relationships in your life? How can you begin to define yourself on your own terms instead of in relation to others?

_____

_____

_____

_____

_____

I set clear boundaries that allow me the breathing room to just be.

DATE: _____

I'M GRATEFUL FOR: _____

I'M MANIFESTING: _____

_____

_____

Think about someone who annoys you or makes you angry. Now, be vulnerable—what qualities do you share with them? How can you change those qualities?

_____

_____

_____

_____

_____

I am a work in progress and
deserve the space and grace
to grow.

DATE: _____

I'M GRATEFUL FOR: _____

I'M MANIFESTING: _____

_____

_____

Anxiety about the future or past can rob us of our present peace. What quick five-minute ritual can you implement throughout the day to be more present in the moment?

_____

_____

_____

_____

_____

I let anxiety flow through me and out of me. Peace is my stronghold.

DATE: _____

I'M GRATEFUL FOR: _____

I'M MANIFESTING: _____

_____

_____

Do you have any preconceptions about femininity? What about being a Black woman specifically? Where did these preconceptions come from? Do they hurt or heal you?

_____

_____

_____

_____

_____

I am my own woman.
I don't have to be every woman.
I am enough.

I'M GRATEFUL FOR: _____

I'M MANIFESTING: _____

_____

_____

How do you feel about manifesting your dream life? Excited? Confused? Overwhelmed? Have you told anyone about your manifestation journey? Who else can support you on this path?

_____

_____

_____

_____

_____

I take ownership over my life, and I attract abundance like never before.

A FINAL NOTE

If you're reading this, show yourself some love. You're on your way to manifesting the beautiful life you deserve, queen! Being a Black woman in our society can be hard, but you decided to delve into your purpose and intention anyway. When it comes to continuing the practice of manifesting a life that you love, I encourage you to grant yourself persistence and patience. Persistence will allow you to stay steadfast in your desires, and patience will allow you to enjoy your present circumstances as you wait for your future.

My charge for you, sis, is to share this reignited power and purpose with other Black women because your voice matters. You are strong, capable, and impactful just as you are. And on this journey, as your voice becomes more emboldened and your spirit becomes even more indomitable, I hope that you help other sisters find freedom and support them on their journeys. Our legacies are tied to each other; we need one another as we walk through this life. I wish you more joy than your hands can carry, and I hope you'll always remember that our ancestors are constantly conspiring in our favor.

RESOURCES

Apps

Balance

Black Girl Meditations by Insight Timer

Exhale

Books

The New Black Woman: Unlocking the Queen Within; Escaping the Mental Prison with Positive Affirmations by J. T. Jennings

Self-Love Workbook for Black Women: Empowering Exercises to Build Self-Compassion and Nurture Your True Self by Rachel Johnson, LMSW, MFT

Podcasts

Black Girl in Om

Black Girl Manifest Podcast

Manifesting While Black Podcast

REFERENCES

Blatchford, Emily. "How Neuroplasticity Can Help You Get Rid of Your Bad Habits." *HuffPost*. November 21, 2017. Huffpost.com/archive/au/entry/how-neuroplasticity-can-help-you-get-rid-of-your-bad-habits_a_23283591.

Bowen, Sarah, and Marlatt, Alan. "Surfing the Urge: Brief Mindfulness-Based Intervention for College Student Smokers." Psychology of Addictive Behaviors: Journal of the Society of Psychologists in Addictive Behaviors. 23, no. 4 (December 2009): 666–671, doi: 10.1037/a0017127.

Conde, Shayna. "Black Women Have Used Self-Affirmation for Centuries. Why Does Instagram Make It Look So White?" *Allure*. February 28, 2022. Allure.com/story/decolonizing-affirmations-black-community-spirituality.

Diekelmann, Susanne, Ines Wilhelm, Ullrich Wagner, and Jan Born. "Sleep to Implement an Intention." *Sleep* 36, no. 1 (January 1, 2013): 149–53. Ncbi.nlm.nih.gov/pmc/articles/PMC3524538.

"Gratitude Letter." *Greater Good in Action*. Accessed September 9, 2022. Ggia.berkeley.edu/practice/gratitude_letter.

Masango, Maake J. S. "African Spirituality That Shapes the Concept of Ubuntu." *Verbum et Ecclesia* 27, no. 3 (2006): 930–43. Ubuntuinstitute.com/images/uploads/concept_of_ubuntu_as_african_religion3.pdf.

Mead, Elaine. "47 Goal Setting Activities, Exercises & Games (+ PDF)." *PositivePsychology.com*. June 1, 2019. Positivepsychology.com/goal-setting-exercises.

Portland Psychotherapy. "Riding the Wave: Using Mindfulness to Help Cope with Urges." *Accessed September 9, 2022.* Portlandpsychotherapy.com/2011/11/riding-wave-using-mindfulness-help-cope-urges.

Pullar, Jess. "The 'Hot Girl Walk' Is Trending on TikTok—but What Exactly Is It?" *Elle.* May 24, 2022. Elle.com.au/culture/what-is-the-hot-girl-walk-27105.

ACKNOWLEDGMENTS

Thank you to my mother, Winone Oliver, and my aunties, Varie Person and Cassandra Quinn—the Black women who helped me find my voice—and to my daddy, Ray Oliver, and my brother, Michael Oliver, my men of few words who love me relentlessly. To the team at Rockridge Press, thank you, with special thanks to my editor, Van Van Cleave, for your immense kindness. To my Yoga and Mahogany family, the journey to revolutionary wellness continues. To my fiancé, Kevin Thomas, my mirror, who celebrated every literary milestone and wiped every tear, I love you and choose you every single day.

ABOUT THE AUTHOR

Ashley R. Oliver, Esq., is a registered yoga teacher, civil rights lawyer, corporate diversity and inclusion director, content creator, and activist. She is the founder of Yoga and Mahogany, a platform for inclusive wellness that encourages self-care as a revolutionary act, particularly for Black women. Find Ashley on social media at @yogaandmahogany.

Printed in the USA
CPSIA information can be obtained
at www.ICGtesting.com
LVHW061021110324
774135LV00027B/247